Stuck in the Spotlight: Tips and Techniques for Overcoming Stage Fright and Mastering Public Speaking

Table of Contents

Introduction

There will always come the time when we need to speak in front of a crowd. Public speaking is an essential part of letting our voices be heard. Whether it's a small group or a huge audience you're speaking in front of, you must be well prepared to let everyone know and understand what message it is that you wish to relay.

However, not everyone is able to speak in front of the public. There are a lot of difficulties that are present in public speaking, some of which are present in specific individuals, particularly those with stage fright, but may not occur with others. Some individuals are rather adept or they just have it in them to speak without fear or anxiety.

Public speaking could be done properly or we can do it badly. The outcome always greatly influences the way people look at the speaker or how they perceive the persons thoughts and behaviors.

It is essential to take precautionary measures before publicly speaking. From the way you dress down to the very movement of your fingers, everything must be accounted for. Not a single detail must be overlooked.

Being a part of the listening crowd is somewhat a practice that we have all been living with. However, being the person on stage having to be heard by many people is like living in an entirely different world. You'd probably encounter a different perspective of things when you're up on that stage conveying your message.

Chapter 1: Putting Success in the Works

A lot of people fail to deliver effective public speaking for several reasons. One of which is the lack of preparation. To be able to come up with great public speaking is to take into account many prerequisites. The first thing to understand about public speaking is that it is the product of skills and preparation combined.

Public speaking is not something that you just do without first being prepared. If you do that, the result on your part would be chaotic. You'd need to leverage your strengths making it possible to overcome the weak points in your delivery. To be prepared, you must ask yourself a couple of questions like:

- What are my strengths?
- What are my weaknesses?
- Do I have all the skills I need?

Explore yourself. Assess the things you have and the things you don't. It would help if you had someone to guide you through this process. Like they always say, "two heads are better than one." First off you need to understand your strengths. Now, these can be anything that you're good at that would help you deliver a better presentation. Having a clear, crisp voice for instance, is one good quality that you could have. If not, you might need to look into that because a great public speaking requires your voice to be heard, not just by the few people fronting you but by everyone across the room. Also, you must consider looking into the things that you don't have. Think of the things that you're not good at. Be honest when you think about this because it's going to help you out a lot. Don't think of it as a bad thing to find yourself lacking but rather think of it as room for improvement. Having a good perspective is a really useful tool in improving yourself.

First up, take a recorder, do a sample presentation and listen to your voice carefully. Try to listen to the recording a couple of times and look for any irregularities or things that you think you should not do. Most often, our tone of voice, choice of words, and the delivery of our sentences mean a lot or it could have a huge impact on the outcome of your presentation.

Saying Things Correctly

When you are going to do a presentation, it help to do some research on your topic. Invest your time on finding the right pronunciation of words and jargon. What you say is totally important. However, the way you say it is equally as important. In a nutshell, diction is a very important factor in a great public speaking. The words you say and how you say them is extremely necessary. Slurring your words or won't do you any good.

When pressed with time and you're just halfway through, you might need to speed up a little bit. Speaking too slow would take up too much time. Speaking too fast, however, will only make it faster for your audience to lose interest and probably be annoyed by your delivery. It's all about pacing, dictation, and clarity. It's when the audience fully grasps and understand each word you say that you can conclude you had a great public speaking experience.

If you're not quite sure on where to start, better begin with the basics. Do some diction exercises to get your tongue in shape. Just like athletes do warm ups before they start a game, or the way singers vocalize before each performance, a good public speaker must also be prepared to speak, and utter words with clarity. If it helps, you could try out some tongue twisters preferably from A-Z. This will get your tongue get used to different words plus enabling your brain to memorize each and every one of them. The main purpose of doing articulation exercises is to set up a pattern of better, more enhanced way of speaking. Plus, it also allows the muscle groups involved in speech to be stretched and strengthened. Although it may sound unnecessary but there will always come a time where you encounter words that are just hard to pronounce especially when trying to pronounce words from a foreign language. Having and honing the ability to speak clearly is essential in public speaking as it mainly involves speech. Other than learning to articulate each word you say, you also need to learn some other public speaking preparations.

Abiding the 3 C's of Public Speaking

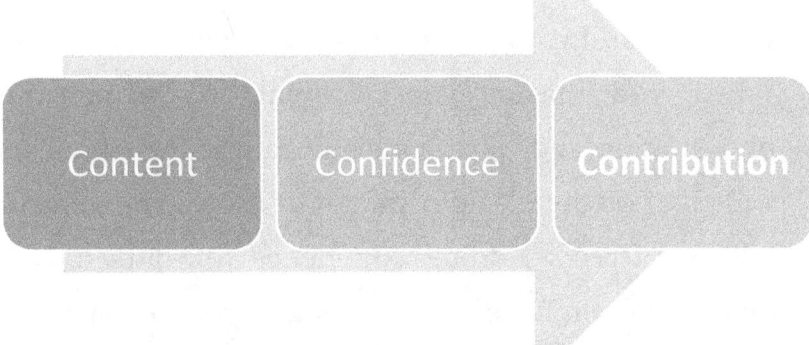

Public speaking is all about conveying a message to your audience and how well you do it. To be able to give a great presentation you must be able to follow the four C's of public speaking:

Content – what will your message be? Be sure not to forget to ask yourself this question. Before anything else, take some time to conceptualize your content. Think about the stuff that you need to discuss and the things that you should not. Although you may have a lot in mind and want to say them all, you might not get that chance to tell everything because it might not be appropriate or it might deviate to a whole new topic. Conceptualize, create, and plan your execution. It's always necessary to map out all the areas you're going to discuss and those you don't

Confidence – gearing up for public speaking demands a huge amount of confidence. Standing in front of a huge crowd alone requires great confidence. Practice is always the best tool to gain confidence. When you master your content, do a mockup presentation and have someone rate it for you. This will give you the idea of whether or not you're going to fail or succeed. Adding confidence to yourself is a matter of faith. Belief that will enable you to do what it is that you need to do. It will also allow you to expand your boundaries daring yourself to go beyond what you're used to and embracing the fact that you could always do more. With that in mind, it's easy to feel confident anytime you want.

Contribution – public speaking is all about conveying a message. However, you must also consider the value of your message and how it can contribute to the betterment of your listeners. It must not only be you who will benefit from your presentation but also for those who have listened. It's just like having a conversation. It can be something that you would forget the next minute or a really good thing that you will carry within you for a very long time.

Chapter 2: Pulling Down the Curtains on Anxiety

When you prepare for a presentation or a speech there will always be a bit of anxiety. This just cannot be helped. We have this built-in mechanism that signals anxiety automatically when we face certain situations, and in this case, public speaking. There's no perfect presentation. On the other hand, when we make a presentation and then realize we made some mistakes, our brain then automatically focuses more on the mistakes rather than the entirety of the speech. This simply confirms such fears and builds up anxiety even more. However, anxiety can be overcome but first you must understand how it happens and how to control it.

What Triggers the Fear of Public Speaking?

Anxiety brought upon by public speaking is basically the fear of embarrassment or being judged. This is because of all the attention that is centered on the speaker at the moment of the presentation. In each presentation, the ideal thing to do would be to speak clearly and loudly. However, the feeling of self-doubt is always present especially with all the attention given to each word you speak. Aside from self-doubt, the fear of embarrassment, or being judged, there are also other causes for public speaking anxiety.

A lot of individuals nowadays are more inclined to stay online somewhere in an enclosed location like their homes. This lack of public interaction causes these individuals to feel discomfort with public speaking and lessens their chances of ever engaging in one.

In this digital age, work becomes less interactive in a physical way. People are using phones, e-mails, and chat applications to convey information. The physical interaction between human to human is starting to disappear as today, the interaction is becoming more of man-machine-man. Although this isn't an alarming thing but future public speakers would find it harder as relative experience is lacking.

It actually doesn't really matter whether or not you're a seasoned public speaker or a younger one. The thing is, modern day life is making interaction with other people seemingly lesser than it was before. However, this only accounts for a small portion of anxiety. There are other causes for anxiety which may have deeper roots and may require different tactics to go about and cure anxiety.

How to Calm your Nerves and Reduce Anxiety

It is common to encounter even the least bit of anxiety as you ready yourself for an upcoming presentation or speech. Even some of the most experienced speakers in the world get a little bit anxious when they are about to hit the stage in front of a really huge crowd. You must not ever expect yourself to be completely free of anxiety. Instead, you must use the anxiety to perform well enough to deliver a great presentation and not the other way around.

In scenarios where public speaking gets the best out of you, it might be time to get yourself some help. The main concern is our tendency to focus all of our attention on the mistakes we make which in turn, makes it hard for us to get over anxiety immediately. It just takes that single mistake to fuel our fears but it's so hard to extinguish that flame.

To be able to break free from your public speaking anxiety, you must make smart decisions prior to speaking, during, and after your presentation. Some individuals get scared and anxious when publicly speaking in front of their friends whom are mixed in a large crowd. That type of anxiety is more of social phobia which may require a different course of action.

Things to do Before Making a Speech

In this instance, what you need to learn is to control or cure public speaking anxiety. It mainly requires a well-though plan and the choice of executing them. Here they are

Prior to your Speech

- Practice, and Practice some more!
- Relax and visualize yourself.
- Don't reject embarrassment, instead, accept it!

During the day of the speech

- Complete muscle relaxation
- Meditate

After the speech

- Write down positive remarks instead of mistakes
- Repeat cycle but this time with lesser anxiety and more preparation

Basically, public speaking anxiety grows bigger as the big date draws nearer. However, there are methods on how you could control anxiety and turn from something destructive into something constructive. First and foremost, practice is extremely essential. Rehearse your lines so you won't forget them. Don't be overconfident thinking that you already know what to say. You'll only become more anxious the moment you forget your lines. It's always a good thing to be confident but taking it to a higher level usually does more harm than good.

Try to think about yourself on that stage giving out your presentation. Think of how you're going to deliver your speech on stage. Visualize yourself thinking of every possible scenario. Take into account everything. Think about how you could perfectly give out your speech and imagine some with a few mistakes and from there come up with a backup plan on how you could easily recover.

Instead of feeling embarrassed, treat your mistakes as your next target. Think of them as the key points that you need to improve. And just bear in mind, nobody's perfect. So, if someone

Chapter 3: Honesty: Be Honest with Yourself

The secret to being a very good public speaker is to ensure that you are always honest with yourself. It is close to impossible for you to be able to speak powerfully if you cannot be truthful with yourself.

Think about this; you are supposed to give a speech about a new program that your company has just launched, and you are supposed to tell your audience how awesome, how effective the program is, but in real sense you know that the program is flawed and you do not like it one it. In such a case, you might be able to deliver a speech based on the speech notes that you have been given, but in the real sense you will struggle with delivering the speech convincingly.

There are some people who can be able to pull off such theatrics with their speeches, but let's be honest, not so many of us are able to lie about a lot of things, especially when you are delivering the speech to a huge audience. Trying to pretend that you do not feel what you really are feeling is an easy lead-up to what psychologists refer to as cognitive dissonance. This is a situation where you end up standing up for two views that are directly opposing one another at the same time, and before long, you will start contradicting yourself. Such a situation can become worse when the audience is already split along hating and loving the program, and in this case, the ones who hate the program can through their responses, will end up influencing your ability to give a good speech in the long run.

When you are honest with what you feel, it becomes easier for you to deliver a really good speech. It is like making peace with the demons in your head. You know they are there, and you know how to keep them at ease. However, if you cannot do this, things can turn from bad to worse in a very short time.

While delivering a speech, always remember that there are members of the audience that come prepared with some really tricky questions, and for this reason you have to be prepared for the worst, just in case things go south at any given time.

Besides, if you keep lying to yourself, you will have effectively managed to brainwash yourself before you even get to meet your audience, and with that you will have lost control of the audience, allowing them enough power to control you and the outcome of the speech.

Pay attention to the audience

There are three important elements of public speaking that will determine how effective you are when you are delivering your speech. These are:

- The speech
- The speaker
- The audience

One of the standout qualities of a good public speaker is their ability to listen to the audience and respond appropriately. What most people do not know about public speaking is the fact that in as much as you are delivering the speech, you also need to be alert so that you can lend the audience a hearing.

Listening to the audience can be taken in different ways, either literally or in an implied manner. Literally speaking, you need to hear out your audience so that you can respond to their concerns, questions and anything else that they may raise during the speech. This is the simpler part because you are basically engaging with the audience based on the spoken word that they are sharing with you.

However, at the same time, a good public speaker needs to be able to pay attention to the implied messages that the audience is sending. These can be anything from gestures to facial and bodily expressions. The main reason why you need to understand these in particular is because the audience will in some cases not be able to outwardly face you and question a few things about your speech, but they will instead show their appreciation or disapproval of your speech through actions. This is especially so if there is a wide gap in superiority between your position in society and the position that the general audience enjoys.

Learning to listen to the audience will enable you learn beforehand how well they are taking to the speech, whether they are bored, or whether it is time for you to switch things up a gear. Rest assured that listening to the audience has everything to do with how successful you will be in delivering the speech.

In order to understand how important it is for you to pay attention to the needs of the audience, you can relate to a situation where someone tried to talk to you, and kept on talking for time on end without a care in the world about what your reaction is. It can be so frustrating because it feels like the interaction is one dimensional, while a good speech is supposed to be all-round, with all the participants involved in one way or the other.

One of the important things that you have to understand about public speaking is that it is not all about you who is delivering the speech, but it is also about the audience.

Chapter 4: Getting your Facts Right

Before you get ready for public speaking, always ensure that you have your facts right. There are some important things that you need to know about in as far as fact finding is concerned. The following are the important things that you have to remember at all times:

How long you are going to be speaking

This is the first thing that you need to know about when preparing for a public speech. The length of time you will spend speaking is important so you can plan ahead. You may come prepared for a 20 minute speech, only to get shocked when you are supposed to deliver an hour's worth of speeches. This will definitely set you back, and can also interfere with your thought process.

Know the audience

Public speech is all about understanding your audience. You have to know beforehand the composition of the audience. It is important to know how many of the support your idea and which ones do not support the idea. There are audiences that can be predetermined early enough, especially in the event that you are about to deliver a speech on a contentious issue.

The time of the speech

It is always a good idea to try and know beforehand the time of the day wherein you will be giving the speech. The importance of knowing the time is because it helps you plan ahead of time not only for the speech you are about to deliver, but to help you anticipate the mood that your audience will be in. This is because naturally, people can be in different moods in the morning as compared to their moods in the evenings.

The nature of the speech program

Understand what the rest of the speech program is all about. This is important to help you decipher how receptive the audience will be when you are giving your speech. It helps to know beforehand whether you are going to be the first, fifth or last speaker, so that you can come prepared to deal with the emotions of the audience after the other speakers have done their thing.

It also helps to know who the other speakers are, because if you are making a speech after President Obama has made his, chances are high that you will really need to be on top of your game. Actually, you will need a miracle to keep the audience in the same emotion as he has, or to sustain their level of anticipation based on the speech that they have just been exposed to.

Getting the answers to these questions will help you determine how to plan your speech, and most importantly how to deliver it in the best way possible.

The bottom line about public speaking is the fact that when you are delivering a speech, you will be delivering the speech to someone, and about something. It is therefore important to know who these people are and what the subject means.

The following are some questions that you will need to ask before you go on to deliver a speech, so that you can plan properly for the same.

- What is the name of the event, the time, venue and date?
- What topic are you supposed to address?
- How long is the speech supposed to last?
- What is the main agenda that the speech is supposed to achieve?
- Is it possible to get access to the main agenda of the speech?
- Who will introduce you, and is it possible if you can send them a prepared introductory note?
- Who do you refer to in the event that you need more information?

If possible, get to know about the useful demographics about the audience. The following are some of the important things that you need to know about your audience.

- How many people will be in the audience?
- The demographics about the audience (the age, occupation, gender, background) – at this point, try to know anything possible that can help you make a difference
- What is their attitude towards the topic?
- Will the audience be allowed to ask questions during the speech or after?
- Will you be allowed to mingle with and socialize with the audience before, during or after the speech is over?

The answers to these questions will go so far in ensuring that you are able to deliver a really good speech, one that the audience will remember for a very long time.

Chapter 5: Public Speaking vs. Conversation

Come to think about it, what is the difference between public speaking and talking? Have you ever thought about it? Public speaking is pretty much talking, the only difference is that you have a bigger audience.

Did you know that public speaking and talking are so similar that it becomes easier for you to slip in a slight public speech into an everyday conversation? You can do it so well that the person you are speaking to might not even be able to notice the difference.

This is all about practice. No one wakes up one day and becomes a good public speaker from nowhere.

Everyone starts from somewhere, and as long as you are willing to give it a try, there is every possibility that you will be able to build up on the little that you have and in the long run perfect your art.

The concept of public speaking and having a conversation is similar, with the only difference being that in public speaking nothing is private, and there is an ultimate goal. Having a conversation can at times be just about making small talk and getting to pass time, but with public speeches, there is always an objective; passing some information, sharing some knowledge and so forth. The most important thing about public speaking is the call to action.

With public speaking there is always something in your mind that you want the listener to do, something you want them to feel, a message you want them to get; in most cases you already have an outcome in your mind, an outcome that is desirable to your immediate cause. Having a normal conversation on the other hand can be open-ended. It might be possible that you have a general goal, but you might not necessarily be trying to convince your friends to do something as is the case with public speaking.

It is easier for you to hone your skills in public speaking by becoming more interactive with your daily conversations as you get to build up your confidence. The following are some simple pointers that can help you set the ball rolling:

- **Plan** – Always plan what you are going to say in the speech ahead of time. This will help you be preemptive and be ready for anything that might come out of your schedule

- **Practice** – Always practice saying what you are going to say in advance, so that you can make sure it feels and sounds right in your mind before you say it out to the audience

- **Clarity of speech** – Speaking clearly is always a prerequisite to perfecting your act in public speaking, because it makes it easier for you to be heard.

- **Confidence** – Always be sure to exude a sense of confidence while you are speaking. Speak slowly and authoritatively

When you are delivering the speech, be sure to be on the lookout for the reaction of the audience. You need to know whether or not you are able to persuade them. Remember that the audience will probably not know that you are taking a keen interest in their reactions, so this gives you an upper hand.

Chapter 6: Simple Rules of Public Speech

From time to time we confuse the conventional rules of writing with the rules of public speaking, and the result can be a disaster. In public speaking, some of the basic rules of writing do not apply, and as a matter of fact in most cases these rules work in the inverse. In writing, you are normally told not to repeat yourself, not to use clichés, or not to start a conversation with conjunctions. We are going to use these three examples to reiterate the difference between public speaking and writing. If you hold on to that school of thought and think about public speaking, all of these rules do apply, but to your benefit, not to your detriment.

In public speaking for example, it helps to repeat yourself. If you want to stress a point, there is no better way to do it other than to repeat the point convincingly until it resonates with the audience. The same applies to the use of conjunctions at the beginning of a sentence. When you do this, you are able to call the audience to attention. This is also a very good way to let the audience know that you are about to make an important point that they should not miss out on. Clichés and formulas always work, depending on how well you can use them, or how effectively you can put them in the middle of your speech. One thing that we have to highlight however, is the fact that overly making such choices can make your speech bland and too predictive.

Listening and reading are two different things, and you should not assume that just because something feels wrong in writing it will automatically feel wrong in speaking. When you are giving a speech, it helps to repeat yourself from time to time. Listeners do not have the luxury that readers have, the luxury of reading a passage over and over and mulling over the meaning.

During public speech, ideas are conveyed to listeners in real time, so in the event that someone does not get to grasp an idea the moment it is being said, there is no way you for them to get it again, unless of course you choose to repeat it.

The interesting thing about repeating an idea is that you need to know your facts well, so that if for some reason someone asks you to repeat a point that you made earlier on, you will not contradict yourself. This is also important because there are some audiences that will be taking notes, so you need to ensure that you never contradict yourself on anything.

Using connectors in public speaking is a very good way to connect your ideas. You can either choose to use your voice, body language or at times a dramatic pause can also come in handy to help you connect the relationship between ideas.

It is important to understand the fact that public speaking is pretty much a mirror to the manner in which we speak from time to time, including the use of conjunctions.

One of the vital points that you have to remember is that when it comes to public speaking, it is good to start your sentences whichever way you want to, as long as it feels natural, and effective.

Always be yourself. When you are giving a speech, it might be easier for you to think about taking the easier way out and pretending to be someone else, but in the long run, you can only be successful with public speaking when you are yourself. Do not mimic someone else, however much you would love to be as good as they are.

When you try to be someone else it becomes easier for you to make mistakes, and these will surely get caught. Be proud of who you are. It does not matter that you are just a beginner at public speaking, or if you have perfected the art, never try to be someone else.

Remember that in as much as you have been doing some research into the audience, some of them might actually take their time to do some digging into the speakers that are going to grace the stage.

Public speaking is the most honest kind of conversation that you can ever come across. When you are speaking to your audience, they will read deep into you, they will see through any lies that you may propagate, and it is for this reason that you need to make sure that you get your facts right all the time.

Thanks to technology, there are members of your audience who are tech savvy who will take a keen interest in searching for facts online to validate your claims. Therefore try not to let anything slip.

The key to a good speech is to do your research into everything, from the audience to your topic, to the venue to the rest of the other speakers that will grace the occasion. You should never leave anything to chance, and in the event that you are not so sure about something, try not to speak convincingly about it.

Final Thoughts

In public speaking, there is nothing like perfection. Even the greatest of public speakers will admit to the fact that from time to time they end up struggling with a few issues here and there. Imagine someone like the president who has had experiences with speeches all over the world getting nervous when they are about to give a speech to school children. This might not sound like a reality to you just yet, but rest assured that it happens.

There is always an expression that has powered through the ages; "good is the enemy of great". We live in a society that is obsessed with achievements and because of this the meaning and inference of this phrase is all too clear. Do not be content with good when you can do great. When you get too comfortable with the good, chances are high that you will never be able to go further than what you have already achieved.

On the other hand, just because you have the opportunity and the ability to experience and enjoy greatness does not necessarily mean that you should pursue greatness. There are so many who have been so good at what they do, but when they decided to pursue greatness they failed at it miserably.

Perfection in public speaking is not a guarantee, but it is something that can be achieved. With the right impetus there is nothing that is out of reach for you, especially if you have the determination. Push and keep pushing yourself until you are able to get to a position where you can deliver a speech at any given time, and to any audience.

In the event that you are seeking perfection, you must also open up to the possibility that you may slip up along the way. This should however not deter you from keeping on. Even the best speakers have failed more than once, and if some of them were to tell you how many times they wanted to opt out, you may be surprised.

In as far as public speaking is concerned it is okay to go after greatness, but first you have to make sure that you have experienced the best there is to goodness. Only punch above your weight when you are sure you can hold your own. Without that things can come crumbling down so fast.

Try not to be too harsh on yourself with the judgments. Judging yourself too harshly will end up hurting your esteem, and before you know it, this can manifest and make you give up on public speaking altogether. On the same note, it is okay to set standards, or to have someone set standards that you can live up to, but when the standards are too high, panic attacks can set in very easily and this might derail your growth process in public speaking.

Always remember this; there is and there will never be anything like perfection in public speaking. Even the best from the Queen to the stand-up comedians have a hard time preparing for speeches and eventually make them look so easy. However, while we all give standing ovations and applaud them for the incredible performance, no one will ever know how fast their hearts race when they imagine getting on stage to deliver their speeches. Perfection is a mirage, do not lose yourself chasing it.

I recognize the struggle that people who have never had to stand infront of a crowd and present a speech have to go through from time to time, but rest assured that all it takes is an initiative, and the will to become better.

Yours sincerely,

David

Other

If there is one thing that any public speaker has to understand, it is the fact that public speaking is never an easy task. It does not matter how well you are at it, every other time you have to endure stage fright. It is important for any practicing speaker to learn to embrace the stress that is associated with public speeches.

As is the case with any challenges in life, the most important thing that will get you through is how well you can learn to cope with it. In the event that you are just starting out, take heart because according to relevant studies on the challenges that speakers face, amateurs and professionals basically go through the same challenges when it comes to public speech.

The sense of anxiety that crowds your ability to get out there and deliver a powerful speech cuts across the board, and perhaps the biggest difference that sets you apart from the professional speakers is the fact that they are in a better position to interpret their anxiety, and use it as a weapon against their audience.

As a beginner, this anxiety can become detrimental to you, perhaps because you do not know yet how to channel your energy and establish a strong connection with the audience from your weak points.

Professionals on the other hand are able to energize the audience even if they start on a low note, as they get to wear off the anxiety.

The notion of stress in public speaking does not necessarily mean that you are going to fail at it, but it is basically an inference to the fact that you are undergoing a lot of pressure. This kind of stress is normal; it is a neutral and acceptable part of life, so do not let it get the better of you.

It is important for you to learn how to overcome some of these challenges because the mere fact that you are struggling with motivation and getting stressed up is not supposed to make you feel terrible about your skills in public speaking. Besides, your level of stress will not add any value to your audience. It does not matter how well or poor you pick up the speech, what matters most is your ability to build on the same and interact with the audience in such a manner that you can impart your speech to them and get them to understand what you are talking about.

You will need to try and overcome this before you can be able to effectively get over things like stage fright. As is the case with any other activity for that matter, you have to do a lot of practice to perfect your act.

The more practice you do, the easier it will be for you to overcome this type of stress, and with time you will be in a good position to learn how to pick up your enthusiasm once you are on stage.

www.ingramcontent.com/pod-product-compliance
Lightning Source LLC
Chambersburg PA
CBHW071013180526
45168CB00003B/1407